Dogs Have Puppies

by Emily J. Dolbear and E. Russell Primm

Animals and Their Young

Content Adviser: Terrence E. Young Jr., M.Ed., M.L.S.
Jefferson Parish (La.) Public Schools, and Janann Jenner, Ph.D.

Reading Adviser: Dr. Linda D. Labbo,
Department of Reading Education, College of Education,
The University of Georgia

Compass Point Books
3722 West 50th Street, #115
Minneapolis, MN 55410

Visit Compass Point Books on the Internet at *www.compasspointbooks.com* or e-mail your request to *custserv@compasspointbooks.com*

Photographs ©: Mark Raycroft, cover, 4, 6, 8; Kent and Donna Dannen, 10, 12, 14, 16, 18, 20.

Editors: E. Russell Primm and Emily J. Dolbear
Photo Researcher: Svetlana Zhurkina
Photo Selector: Linda S. Koutris
Designer: Bradfordesign, Inc.

Library of Congress Cataloging-in-Publication Data

Dolbear, Emily J.
   Dogs have puppies / by Emily J. Dolbear and E. Russell Primm III.
      p. cm. — (Animals and their young)
   Includes bibliographical references (p.   ).
   ISBN 0-7565-0060-5 (hardcover : lib. bdg.)
      1. Puppies—Juvenile literature. [1. Dogs. 2. Animals—Infancy.] I. Primm, E. Russell, 1958– . II. Title. III. Series.
SF426.5 .D65 2001
636.7'07—dc21   00-011502

Table of Contents

What Are Puppies?

Puppies come in all shapes and sizes. In fact, there are more than 300 kinds, or **breeds**, of puppies. Dogs that are a mix of breeds are called **mutts** or **mongrels**.

Some dogs are pets and some dogs work. They herd farm animals or help blind people to get around. This book is about pets—the kinds of dogs that live with people. Did you know that dogs have lived with people longer than any other kind of animal?

◄ A West Highland terrier puppy

What Happens before Puppies Are Born?

Nine weeks after a female dog mates with a male dog, puppies are born. A mother dog may have five puppies at one time. A newborn group of puppies is called a **litter**. A large dog may have a litter of twelve puppies!

Four puppies were born in this litter of pugs.

What Happens after Puppies Are Born?

Newborn puppies can't see or hear. They cuddle up with each other to stay warm. They spend most of their time sleeping.

Puppies need their mother for everything. She feeds them and keeps them warm and safe. She also cleans her puppies. When they are three weeks old, the puppies begin to change. Now they can walk, bark, and wag their tail.

◀ This newborn golden retriever can't see or hear.

How Do Puppies Feed?

It takes about ten to fifteen days for newborn puppies to open their eyes. But they can **nurse**, or drink milk from their mother, soon after they are born.

Puppies stop nursing when they are about six weeks old. Then they start to eat solid food.

◀ A Samoyed mother nurses her pups.

What Does a Puppy Look Like?

Puppies may look like their parents—only smaller. But adult dogs can look very different from one another.

Dogs may have short, medium, or long hair. Mexican hairless dogs have almost no hair at all! Some dogs may have long legs and some have short legs. All dogs have five toes on the front paws and four toes on the back paws. And they may have ears that stand up or ears that hang down.

Some dogs are very strange looking!

What Colors Are Puppies?

Puppies can be black, brown, white, tan, or golden. They can also be a mix of colors. Dogs of the same breed may be different colors. For example, a Labrador retriever may be yellow, black, or brown. A litter of mixed-breed puppies can also be different colors.

Puppies can change color too. Dalmatian puppies are white for the first month. Then they get black or brown spots on their coats.

◄ Sometimes puppies from the
same litter are different colors.

What Do Puppies Do and Eat?

Puppies can begin to play with humans when they are about six weeks old. All puppies need exercise and attention. They want to please their owners. Active puppies can become well-behaved dogs when they are trained. A dog's training can begin when it is six months old.

Puppies eat three times a day for the first six months. Adult dogs eat only once a day. Puppies need to eat the proper dog food. It's not healthy for a dog to eat the food you eat. Both dogs and puppies need plenty of fresh water.

◄ A puppy meets a new friend.

What Happens As a Puppy Grows Older?

Puppies like to spend more time alone as they grow older. They talk by growling or barking. They like to dig holes in the dirt and bury things, such as bones. Sometimes they chase their own tails for fun or exercise. And they still need lots of sleep.

Dogs have a very good sense of smell. They can hear better than people can. However, they have a poor sense of taste. A dog will chew on or eat almost anything.

A Jack Russell terrier digs after a rodent.

When Is a Puppy Grown Up?

A dog reaches its full size when it is one or two years old. Chihuahuas may weigh as little as 1 pound (0.45 kilogram). Saint Bernards weigh up to 180 pounds (82 kilograms). Most adult dogs weigh between 9 and 135 pounds (4 and 61 kilograms).

Small dogs usually live longer than large dogs. A Great Dane may live to be eight or nine years old. Smaller dogs often live ten to fifteen years or more. Owning a dog is a great responsibility. But the rewards of having a furry friend can be even greater!

◀ Eventually puppies look like their parents.

Glossary

breed—a certain kind of dog or other animal

litter—a group of animals born at one time to the same mother

mongrels or mutts—dogs with parents from different breeds

nurse—to drink milk produced by the mother

Did You Know?

- Dogs are related to wolves.

- Studies say that when people pet a dog, their heartbeat and blood pressure go down.

- When dogs get hot, they pant. The saliva that drips from their tongue helps them cool off.

- It is not always true that puppies with big paws grow to be big dogs.

Want to Know More?

At the Library

De Bourgoing, Pascale. *Dogs*. New York: Scholastic, 1999.

Driscoll, Laura. *All about Dogs and Puppies*. New York: Grosset & Dunlap, 1998.

George, Jean Craighead. *How to Talk to Your Dog*. New York: HarperCollins Juvenile Books, 2000.

On the Web

American Kennel Club, Kids' Corner

http://www.akc.org/love/dah/kidskorn/spring00/spring2000_index.html

For a newsletter that educates children about responsible dog ownership

Dog World Magazine

http://www.dogworldmag.com/

For information about dog breeds, training, nutrition, and behavior

Through the Mail

American Kennel Club

260 Madison Avenue

4th Floor

New York, New York 10016

To get information about purebred dogs or find a dog club near you

On the Road

The Dog Museum

1721 South Mason Road

St. Louis, MO 63131

314/821-3647

To visit a museum about the history of dogs

Index

About the Authors

Emily J. Dolbear has been an editor for Franklin Watts, Children's Press, and The Ecco Press. She now works as a freelance writer and editor. Dolbear lives in Chicago with her husband and son.

E. Russell Primm has worked as an editor for more than twenty years. He has been editorial director for Ferguson Publishing Company and for Children's Press and Franklin Watts. He now heads Editorial Directions, a book-producing and consulting company. He lives in Chicago.